Hawaiian Coloring Book: Escape to an Island Paradise

W0231505

Hi everyone,

Thank you so much for purchasing this coloring book. I hope you enjoy it!

I have a special surprise for you…

Claim your gift here: https://bit.ly/2K58AtH

Thanks so much and happy coloring!

© 2018 Megan Swanson

All Rights Reserved.

This book or parts thereof may not be reproduced in any form, stored in any retrieval system, or transmitted in any form by any means—electronic, mechanical, photocopy, recording, or otherwise—without prior written permission of the Publisher

Color Test Page

Color Test Page

TIKI

TIKI
BAR

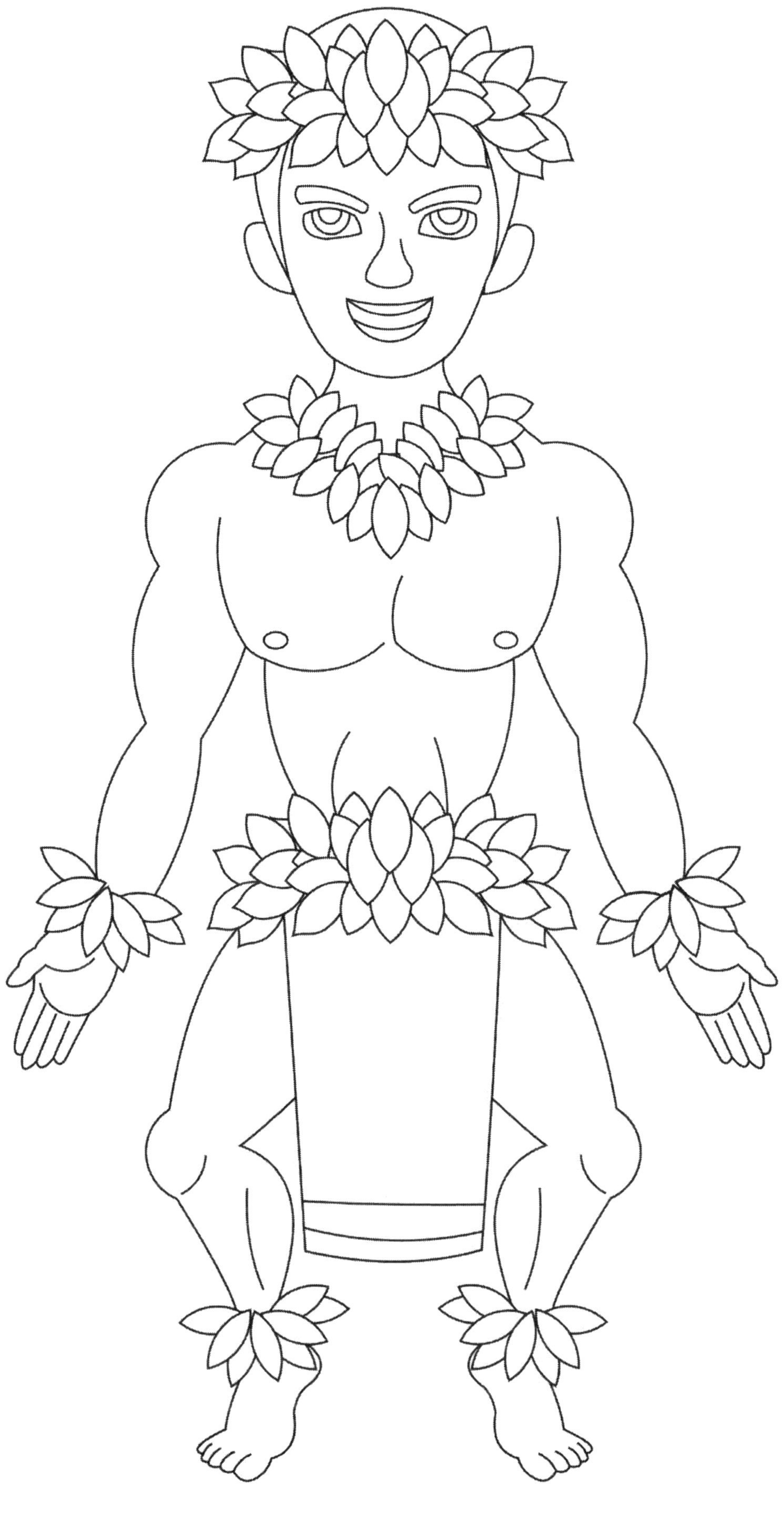

Aloha

Printed in Great Britain
by Amazon

63646190R00038